On Stage!

by Christopher Goldston
Editing and Practice Strategies by Helen Marlais

THE F·J·H MUSIC COMPANY INC.
Frank J. Hackinson

Production: Frank J. Hackinson
Production Coordinators: Joyce Loke and Philip Groeber
Art Direction: Terpstra Design
Cover Art Concept: Helen Marlais
Cover Illustration: Keith Criss
Engraving: Tempo Music Press, Inc.
Printer: Tempo Music Press, Inc.

ISBN 1-56939-663-9

About the Composer

Christopher Goldston holds a Master of Music degree in piano performance and pedagogy from Northwestern University, and a Bachelor of Music degree in piano performance from the University of North Carolina–Greensboro. He lives in Chicago, Illinois, and has taught at Sherwood Conservatory of Music and Harper College.

In 1991, Mr. Goldston received the National Federation of Music Clubs Lynn Freeman Olson Composition Award for his first composition, *Night Train*. Since then, he has written numerous pieces for piano, voice, and chamber ensemble, including *Thesis for Wind Quintet*, which won the 1993 North Carolina State Music Teachers Association Collegiate Composition Contest.

Mr. Goldston has taught piano for over ten years and enjoys composing and arranging pieces for his students. Many of them have created pieces of their own under his guidance and have received top prizes in state competitions. Mr. Goldston has also served as chair of the composition contest for Illinois State Music Teachers Association and MTNA East Central Division.

About the Editor

Dr. Marlais is an Associate Professor of Piano at Grand Valley State University in Grand Rapids, MI, where she directs a comprehensive piano pedagogy program and coordinates all of the group piano programs. Marlais' active performance schedule includes concerts throughout North America, Europe, and Asia, and her travels abroad have also included performing and teaching at the leading conservatories and festivals in Italy, France, Lithuania, Hungary, Turkey, and China. She is the Director of Keyboard Publications for The FJH Music Company, and her articles can be read in the major keyboard journals.

Table of Contents

Which intervals are used the most in this piece? _____ and _____.
Find and circle the intervals of a fourth.
Then place a star above the only interval of a fifth. Prepare this interval as well.

Focus on listening to all of these different intervals while you play the piece.

A Wild Ride

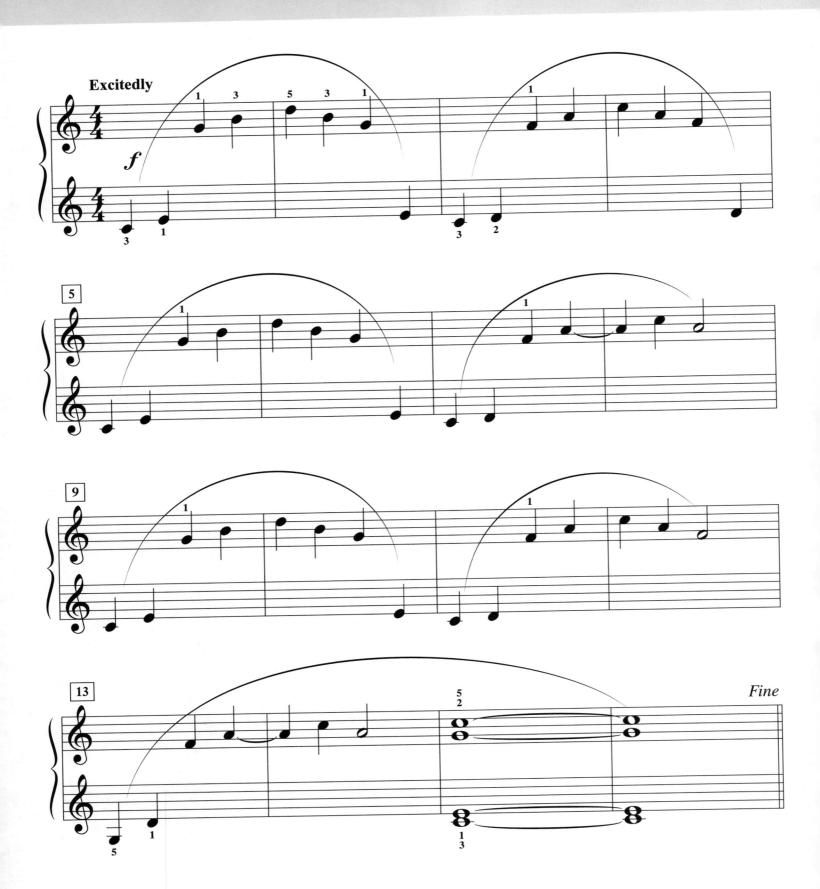

FF17

Find and block (play together) every interval of a fifth. What do you notice about your right hand and left hand thumbs?

Misty Lagoon

Slowly
Both hands one octave higher throughout

Hold right (damper) pedal down throughout

* *loco* means "play as written," not an octave higher or lower.

FF170

An octave is the distance between eight keys.
Notice the octaves in measures 1-6.
Take an extra look at measures 7-8 and 17-18.
What are these intervals?
_____ and _____

Stargazing

F1708

A whole-tone scale is made up of notes that are whole steps apart. With 2 brackets [ ], mark the seven measures where the whole-tone scales are. Plan them carefully before you begin.

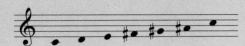

Barn Dance

With energy

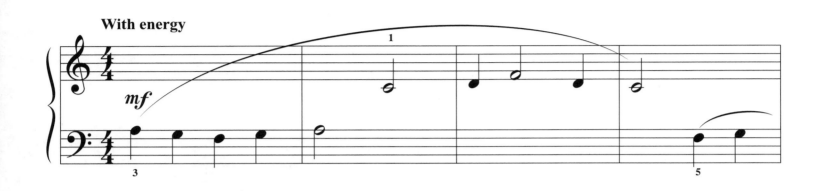

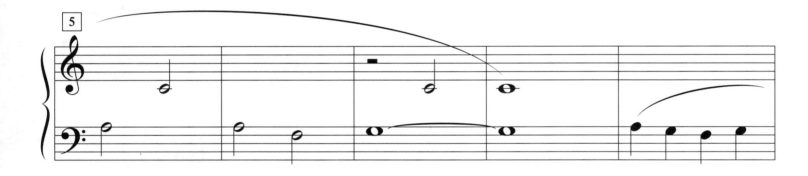

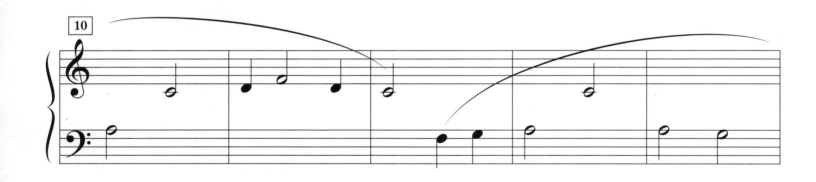

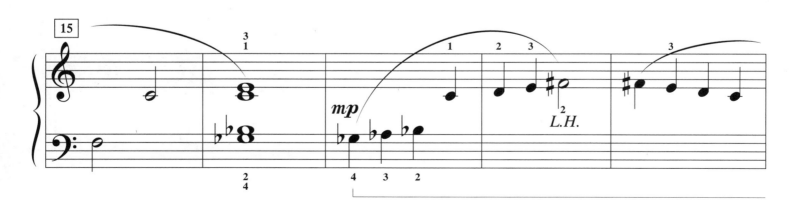

FF170

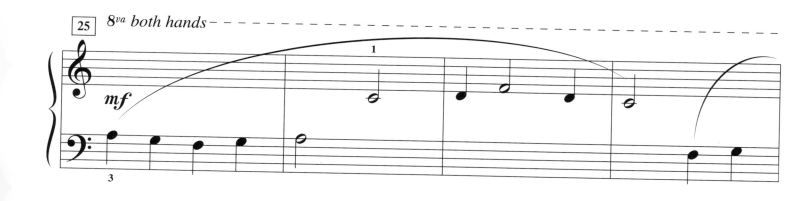

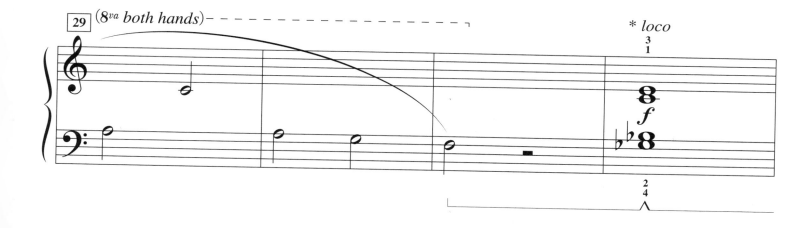

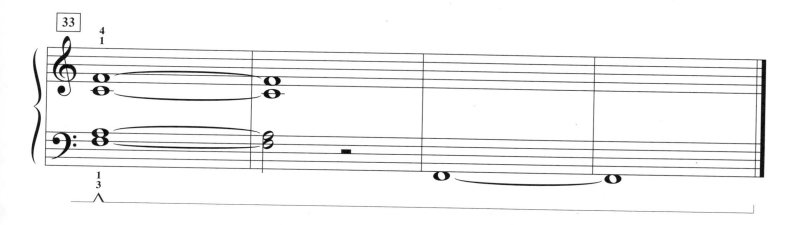

* *loco* means "play as written," not an octave higher or lower.

This piece is made up of whole-tone scales. Just looking at the keys and your hands, can you play a one-octave whole-tone scale beginning on C? Then can you play one starting on C♯?

In the score, circle all of the right-hand groups of whole-tone black keys. Then find them on the keyboard and play them, blocked (notes played together.) Now find and block all the left-hand groups of whole-tone white keys.

In which two measures does the right hand play *white-key* whole-tone groups and your left hand play *black-key* whole-tone scale groups? _____ and _____.

Waves of Fog

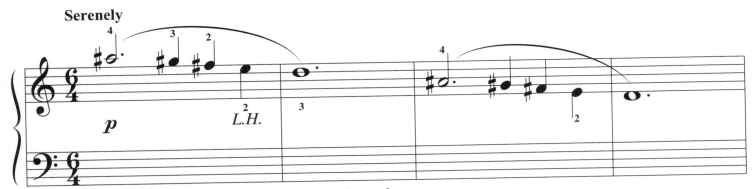

Hold right (damper) pedal down throughout

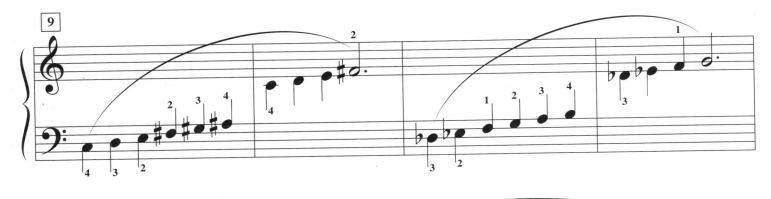

FF1708

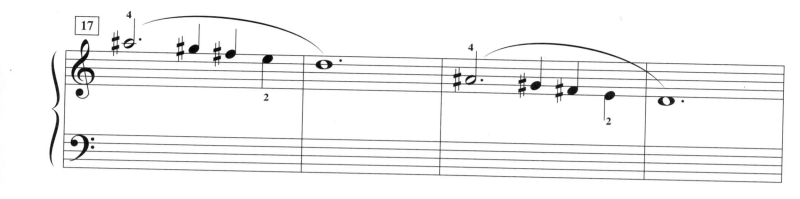

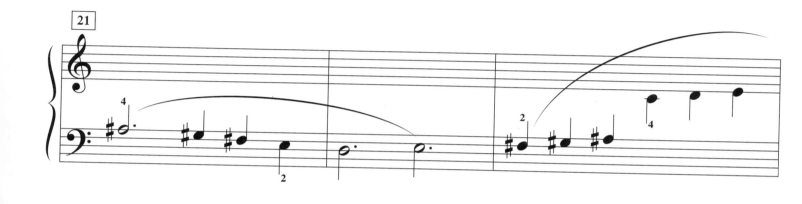

For an even "foggier effect" on an acoustic grand piano, place one or two heavy books quietly on the bottom keys of the piano, letting those strings vibrate as you play this piece.

An interval of a third looks like this:

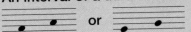 or

How many notes are skipped in a third? _____
Find and block (play together) all of the triads
in this piece. What do you notice about your thumbs? Find and circle all of the intervals that are *not* thirds.
Prepare these before you start the piece.

Brilliant Rainbows

Hold right (damper) pedal down throughout

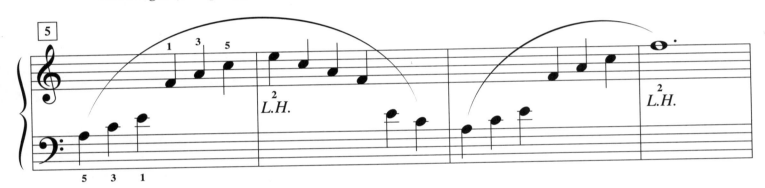

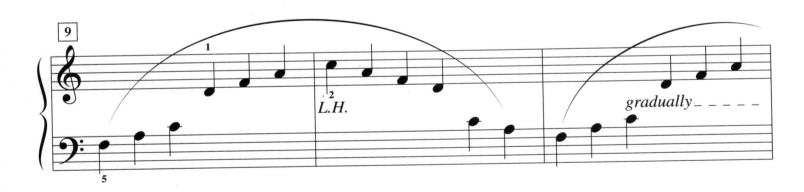

FF170

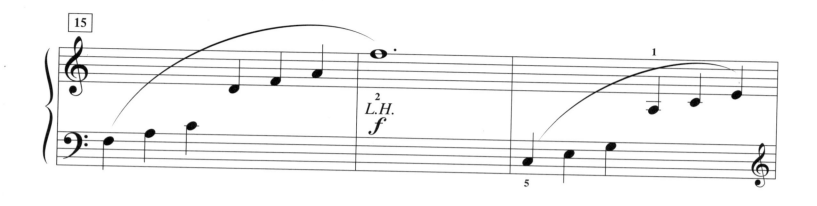

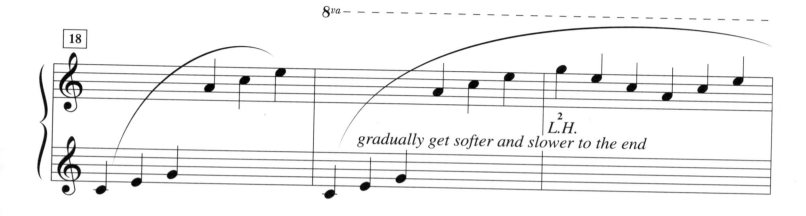

gradually get softer and slower to the end

Look at the intervals in the first line.
Mark in your score where you see the same
intervals again. Look at the left-hand part.
Block (play together) the fifth in measure 5.
Then block the second in m.7. Block all the
other intervals you see in the left hand.

Rock-a-bye

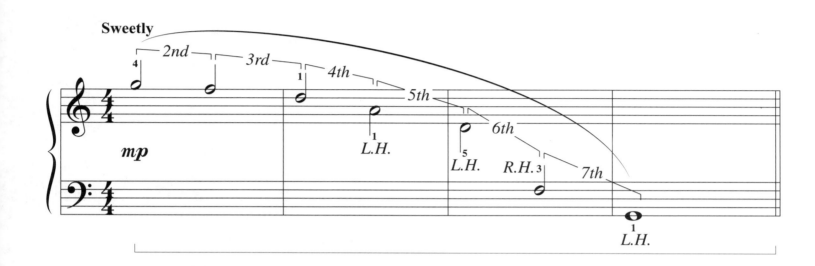

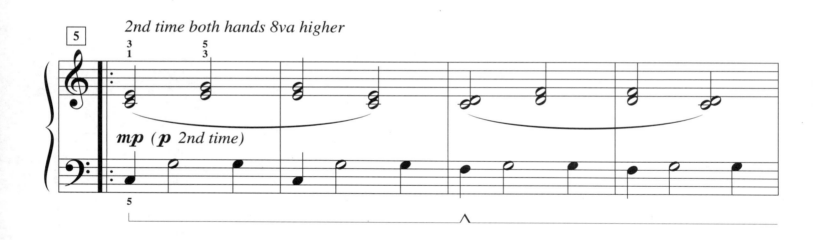

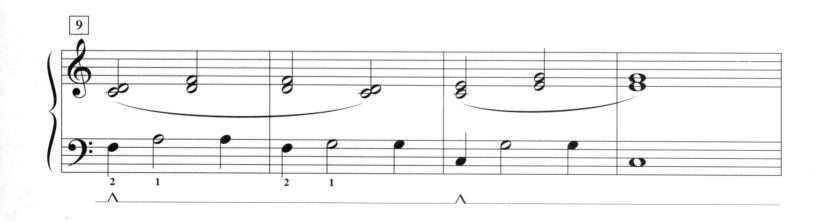

FF170

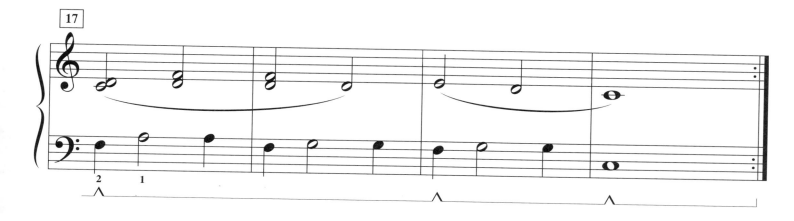

loco

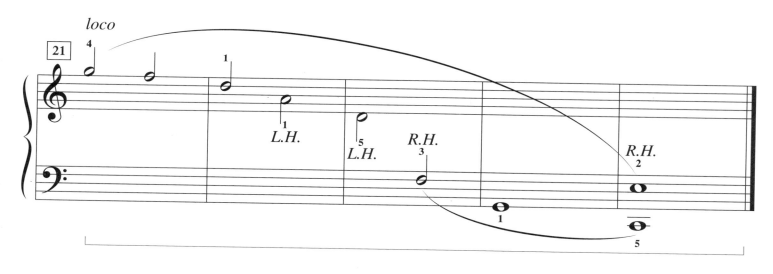

L.H.

L.H.

R.H.

R.H.

This piece is mostly made up of whole steps (m. 1-7). The _____ hand plays the black keys. The _____ hand plays the white keys. Plan the chords in the last three measures carefully. The "giant flat" indicates that all notes on the staff are played as flats (on the black keys).

Mary's Dream

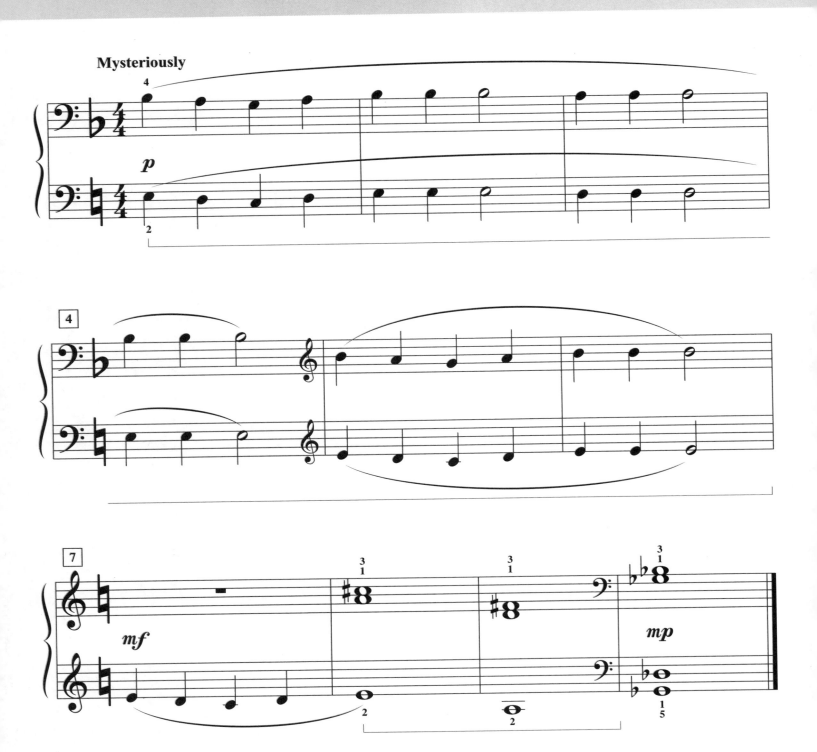

FF170

Play the first two notes of the piece, hands together. This is an interval of a sixth. Find, circle, and play all of the sixths throughout this piece.
Then find the only fifth. Which measure is it in? _____

Aunt Rhody's Goose

Find and play all of the intervals of a fourth in this piece. Are they melodic or harmonic fourths?

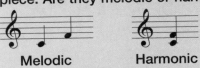

Melodic   Harmonic

(Circle the correct answer.) Then find all the thirds, circling them in the score.

Smooth Sailing

FF17

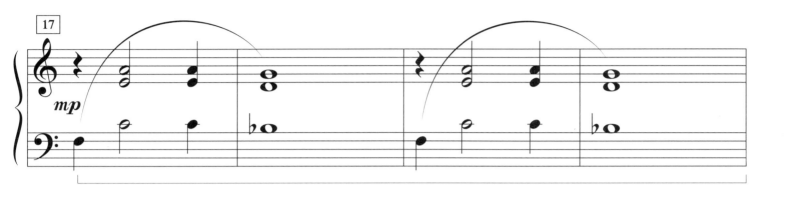

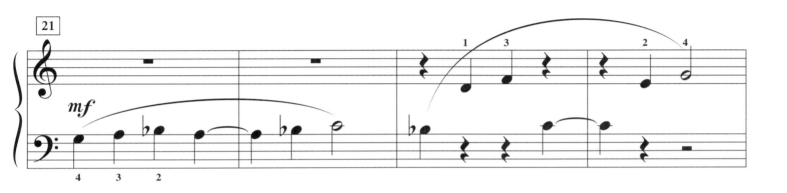

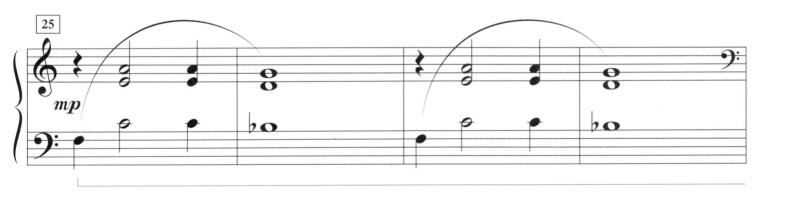

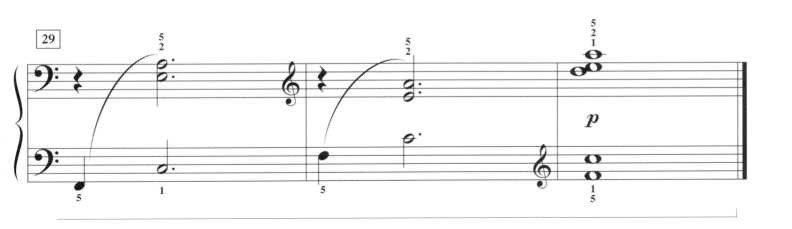

There are half steps, whole steps, seconds, thirds, fourths, fifths, and octave intervals in this piece!

Can you explain by pointing to the notes which intervals are which? If you can, your teacher will place a lightening bolt on the line! _____

Twister

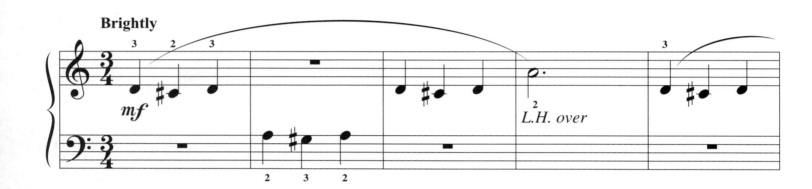

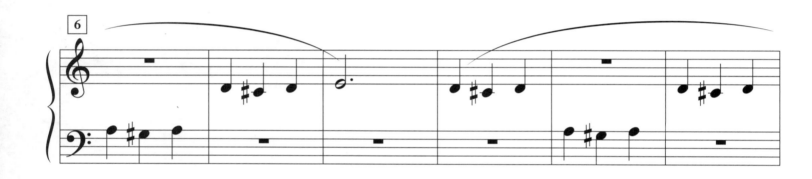

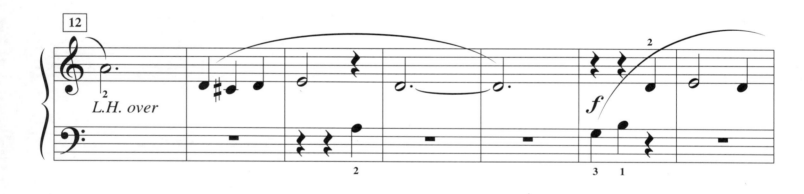

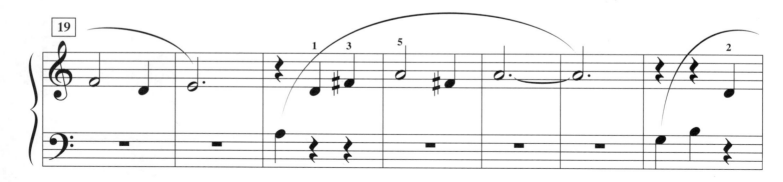

FF17

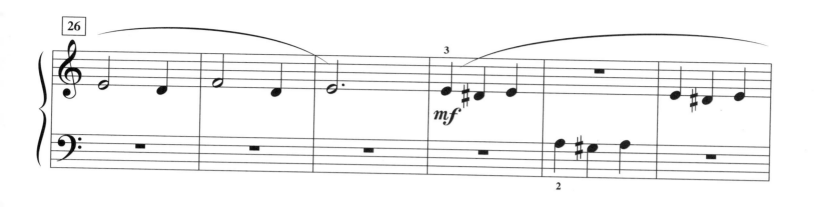

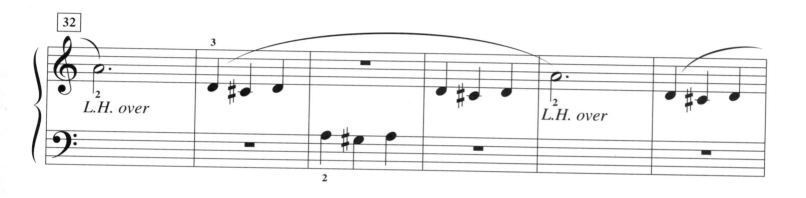

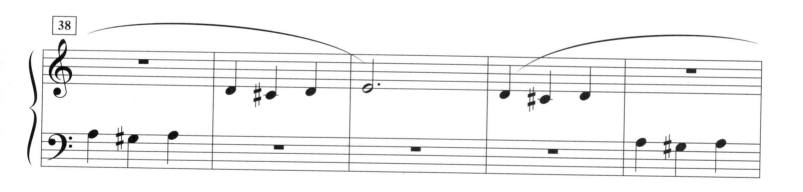

There are many triads in this piece, all played by your right hand.
For example:

The Haunted Clock

These three notes form a triad, and the triad is made up of which intervals?:   seconds   thirds
(circle the correct answer).

Block (play together) all three notes of the triad. Do you notice that ALL of them form an E MINOR TRIAD?

Steadily flowing

L.H. (bring out the L.H. like bells)

hold pedal down until m. 33

Copyright © 2007 The FJH Music Company Inc. (ASCAP).
International Copyright Secured.   Made in U.S.A.   All Rights Reserved.

FF170

Like bells

Find, circle, and block
(play together) all of the fifths.
Play them strongly with
relaxed wrists.

Daybreak in the Canyon

FF17

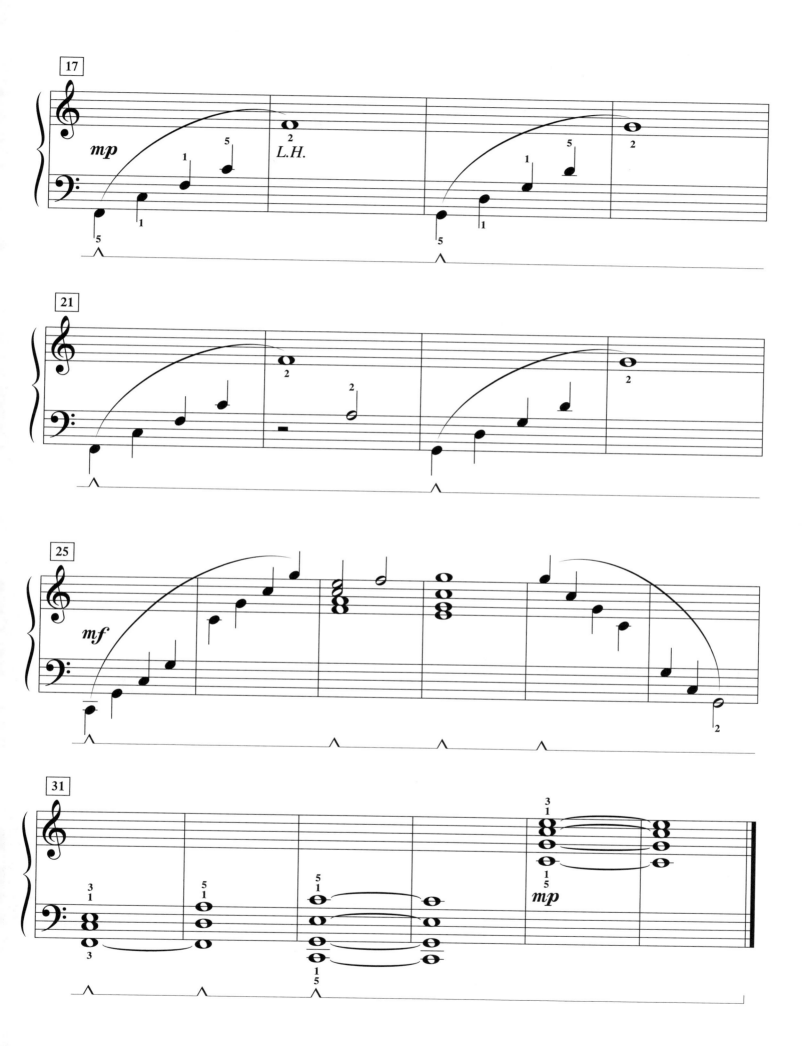

This piece is based on intervals of seconds and thirds.
Find and circle the thirds in your score and block them
(play together) so that you know what they feel like
under your fingers.

Helpful hint: You can count 7 beats/measure like this:

Mark the counting in your score before you begin and the piece will be easy to count!

Busy Beaver

With excited rhythm

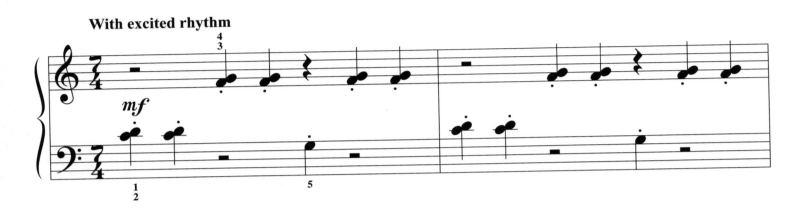

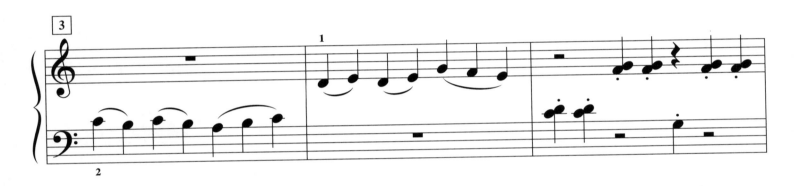

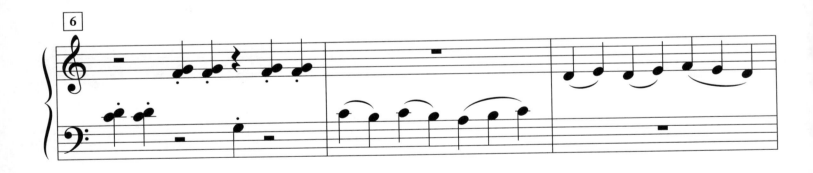

FF17

Little Dictionary

blocking a way to identify melodic chords and intervals, and to play them together, in a vertical (up and down) manner.

dolce an Italian term for "sweetly."

half step an interval between two adjacent keys on the piano, or two keys next to each other.

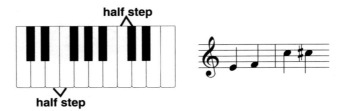

interval is the distance between any two notes.

2nd =

3rd =

4th =

5th =

loco means "play as written," not an octave higher or lower.

moderato an Italian term for a steady, unhurried tempo.

molto ritardando (molto rit.) an Italian term meaning "slowing down a lot."

triad a three-note chord with a root, a third, and a fifth.

whole step an interval made up of two half steps. One key (black or white) is always skipped in a whole step.

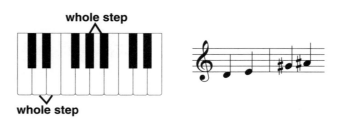

whole-tone scale a scale made up of *only* whole steps. See pieces on pages 8, 10, and 16.